The NEW AGILE MANAGER

By Joseph Flahiff

Seattle Washington

2017

Copyright © 2017 by Joseph Flahiff

All rights reserved. Except as permitted under the United States Copyright Act of 1976, no part of this publication may be reproduced or distributed in any form or by any means. Alternatively, stored in a database or retrieval system, without the prior written permission of the publisher.

Thanks to my wife Jeanne for her unending support and encouragement. Sameer Bendre, Michael Wolf, and Matt Kramer for your input and edits. You made this a better book than when it could have otherwise been. I am forever grateful.

THE NEW AGILE

MANAGER
BY JOSEPH FLAHIFF

Introduction

Hi, I am Joseph Flahiff, and I am excited to have you start this book, *The New Agile Manager*. First, a little bit about me. I am about 47 years old right now as I am writing this book. I am also the author of *Being Agile in a Waterfall World*. I am lucky enough to be married to my best friend Jeanne, and together we have three daughters, all of them delightful in their own ways. They are 18, 14 and 10 years old. We live up in the Seattle area, the beautiful Pacific Northwest and love it.

I have been a traditional and Agile project leader and organizational trainer and coach since the early 2000s. I started my Agile career in 2006 by taking a class from Ken Schwaber, the co-creator of Scrum. The whole story is longer than that, but it was a great class, one I will never forget. This book is not about me. It is about you.

This book may be a little bit different from normal books you have read. It is meant to be very practical and tactical, with advice and actions you can implement right away. We are not just going to be theoretical and talk about how things should work. I want to talk about what you can do right away to change your role as a manager in an Agile organization.

I will help you define what the role of an Agile Manager is, I will help you understand the role that you play. After you understand the role, I will teach you three key skills that you can start using right away.

Finally, we will talk about how you can grow and move beyond just these basic things, but I will share that with you toward the end of the book.

One last thing. I am not in any way a dogmatist. I am a pragmatist. When I see people trying to implement the "standard" way of doing something, but it causes them to do ridiculous things. It bugs me. Often becoming agile is a radical shift, other times it is a course correction. In either case. Try out the ideas, but do not be dogmatic. Test, and experiment with the concepts. What I am telling you has been tried in many organizations and often shows great results. However, if you try it and it does not work, Take what does and drop what does not. It is ok not to follow the rules.

Ok, Are you ready? Then let's dive right in.

Contents

INTRODUCTION	v
THE NEW AGILE MANAGER	1
HIDING OUT IN THE OPEN	9
TIME FOR SOMETHING NEW	11
MANAGERS AS COACHES	27
3 CORE SKILLS OF NEW AGILE MANAGERS	29
THE COACHING MIND	31
POWERFUL QUESTIONS	39
5 STEP COACHING CYCLE	47
WHAT'S NEXT?	57

THE NEW AGILE MANAGER

Managers are the single highest impact person on an employee. Every day you touch the lives of the one, two, thirty, fifty maybe even hundreds of people that you manage.

You have it in your power to change lives. This book will help you make the most of that opportunity.

If you are an Agile manager, if you are a manager in the middle of an Agile transformation or if your organization has already made that shift, I am about to save you a ton of serious frustration. I am going to make the process easier. The ideas in this book have saved hundreds of thousands, even millions of dollars for some organizations.

Over the past decade, I have helped organizations become Agile. I prefer the word "nimble" over agile because the term agile has just way too much baggage with it. Over the years, I have helped many organizations go from traditional waterfall practices to becoming an Agile organization. The process is pretty standard. Most organizations go through the same way. I will go through it step by step for you in another chapter. First, I am just going to share a little bit of my story.

As I have helped organizations, I have seen amazing things happen in them. I have seen people come to life. I had walked through offices where the people were down and depressed when I first arrived. They would walk down the hall with their eyes downcast. After a couple of months of working with them it is not unusual for someone to walk up to me and say, "Joseph, I just wanted to say thank you. You have changed my life." Alternatively, "I used to hate coming to work, and it is like working in a different place now. The place is new. It is different. The people are different. The feel of the organization is different." That is significant. That will get you out of bed in the morning

However, over the years one thing that has never really sat well with me and that is, *how managers are handled*.

Conflicting goals

A lot has changed since the beginning of the agile movement. You could trace that history back to when Ken Schwaber and Jeff Sutherland co-presented a paper on the Scrum Method in 1995. You could also trace the roots back to a paper written in 1989 titled, *The New New Product Development Game*. You can also trace it back through Lean, but that is another book. The management context in the late mid-80's and early 90's was different than it is now. Back then we were in the early-middle stages of the Electronics and Technology revolution. You may not be aware that there have been three industrial revolutions so far:

1. Power and Machines
2. Assembly Line
3. Electronics and Technology

The emergence of lightweight development practices, which were the start of the Agile Movement was happening around the beginning of the Electronics and Technology revolution. People were just learning what it meant to work with information as a product as opposed to working with an actual object as the product, e.g., a car, a desk or dishwasher. When you are making a thing, there is product in front of you, and that takes one set of management tools and techniques. It takes a whole different set of methods and mental models when you are dealing with information and the creative process that it takes to look at, analyze, design, build, and create in a technology environment.

If you are building a new product, a piece of software, website, or business model, you need different management and leadership techniques and styles. They need updating from those used in the manufacturing assembly line industrial revolution, which was the second industrial revolution started back in the turn of the prior century, the 1900s, '20s, and '30s.

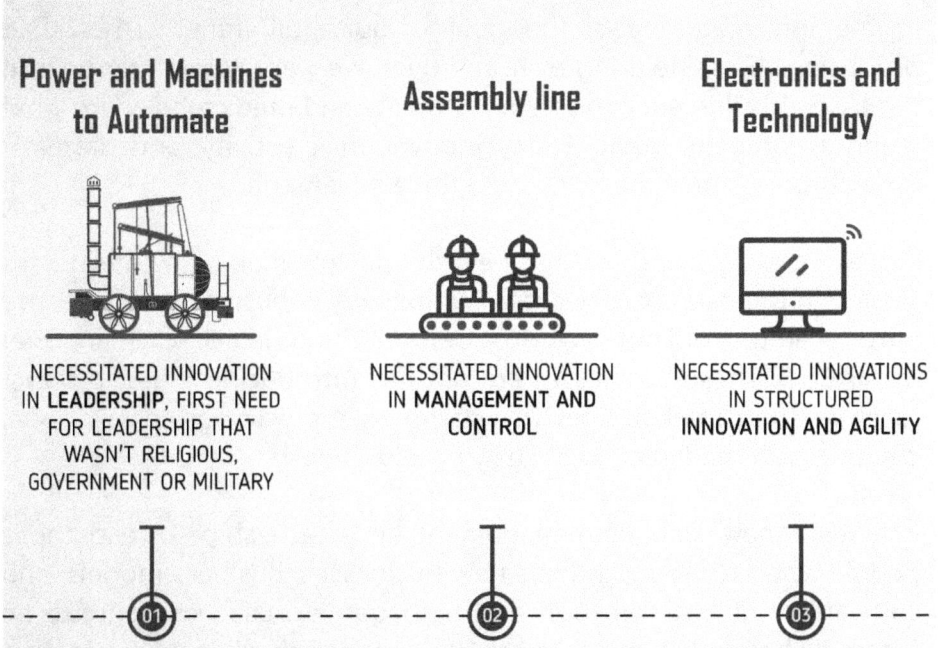

"The First Industrial Revolution took place from the 18th to 19th centuries in Europe and America. It was a period when mostly agrarian; rural societies became industrial and urban. The iron and textile industries, along with the development of the steam engine, played central roles in the Industrial Revolution."[i] In the first Industrial Revolution, we saw the first instance of a need for widespread business leadership theory. At the time one prevalent theory was The Great Man theory. In this theory, it was believed, among other things, that leaders are created by the will of God, and by way of natural, inborn characteristics.

In the second Industrial Revolution, the goal of the assembly line was to create the same product repeatedly and consistently every-single-time. The predominant management approach needed to reduce process variation and create consistent products. For this goal, the command and control model seemed to be well suited. Leaders would figure out the best most optimal version of doing a task and then make everyone do it that way. They were treating the people much like the other pieces of equipment in the factory as if they were very specialized units of mechanization. Strict control was the order of the day.

In the information age, the goal is quite different. Rather than producing the same thing over and over, we want something new. In the assembly line era consistency, stability and predictability are what made a company great. Today innovation, creativity, and dramatic breakthroughs give the key competitive advantage.

Today we are looking for that new thing. How many new businesses started in the past three years? How many new business models were introduced that did not even exist before? Things like Blockchain, Uber or Air B&B. These businesses are not just introducing a new product to an existing market. They are changing the way business is done, creating new markets and destroying old ones.

It takes a new kind of management and leadership to lead those people who are creating these new businesses, business models, and software products. The tools and management used to optimize an assembly line to eek out as much efficiency as possible while creating a product that was cheap enough to manufacture and just good enough that people will buy it, these are not the right tools for this new world of innovation and market disruption.

> *"The world is changing very fast. Big will not beat small anymore. It will be the fast beating the slow."* Rupert Murdoch

Leading a creative and disruptive organization takes a management approach that encourages deviation, the inspiration that allows new ideas, creativity, speed, and the individuality of the employees to come through and shine in all its glory.

In the mid-**1990s there was a mismatch between leadership style and the goal of the business.** There was the leadership style of rigid optimization of processes for consistent delivery of predictable products, and there was the goal of the business, to be adaptive and innovative. Enter the Agile Movement.

Some say Henry Ford said, "Why is it every time I ask for a pair of hands, they come with a brain attached?" That was the perspective of leadership in the assembly line era. Today, in creative work of the information age, there is a conflict. The people who developed agile were creating an approach where they could be creative and expressive. To do that, they had to get the command and control management style out of the way.

As a way of illustrating the conflict, we would tell the story of the chicken and the pig. It was standard fare in agile training until about 2013 or 2014. The story goes something like this. A chicken and a pig were talking one day...

Chicken: Hey Pig. We should open a breakfast restaurant!

Pig: Hum. That sounds good. What should we call it?

Chicken: I say we call it "Ham and Eggs!"

The pig thinks for a moment and says,

Pig: No thanks.

Chicken: Why not Pig, it is a great idea!

Pig: Because I would be committed, and you'd only be involved.

The gist of the story is that the only people invited to team meetings should be those with skin in the game. Since managers "Do not do anything that contributes to the product," they do not have any skin in the game so they should go away. Yes, I have actually said this myself. Not recently but I did say it back then. Remember, though, at that time, managers were trying to strictly control people and processes, as if people were assembly lines, *while at the same time* telling them be creative and innovative. It just does not work that way. You cannot just tell someone to be creative. They have to feel safe.

Most people do not use the Chicken and Pig story today because it is no longer needed. However, you still get the sentiment as an undercurrent in teaching from some agile trainers today. They will talk about managers as being unnecessary, as not contributing, and as outsiders.

Most Agile trainers have three core items that they say that managers need to:

- Stop assigning work.
- Stop asking for status reports
- Stop coming to meetings

Each of these were considered core responsibilities of managers in the command and control model, with the ultimate goal of creating consistency and predictability. I used to say the same things. Until recently.

Stop assigning work was one of the fundamental things that a manager did because managers were the ones who knew the work, who had the skills and knew where to put the right hands. So, assigning work was one of the core job functions of a manager. They spend much time figuring out whom to assign where, what work they should be assigned to take over, how to train them so that they can assign new work in the next phase.

Stop asking for status reports was the second thing we told managers because the team should not be bothered with status reports. If the team has created a project backlog and a status board that visually depicts the status of the project, then you, Mr. or Ms. Manager, should be able to look at that board and see what that status is without having to distract the employee from doing that work. Just do not distract the team members from doing their job. Let them self-organize and take on this work, and they will show you what they are doing with a working product at the end of a short period.

Typically today, the scrum, sprint length is either one or two weeks. So, if it is such a short period, then you should not have to be asking for status that often. Besides, you can look at the Scrum board or the Kanban board and see where we are in progress. It is easy to see.

Stop coming to meetings, is the third directive to managers. Coaches did not want managers to come so that the teams would feel safe. Managers at that time were indoctrinated in a strong command and control philosophy. It was believed (and often the actual case that) managers did not understand how to encourage collaboration; there were not many people preaching the models that are necessary to encourage engagement and creativity (e.g. Simon Sinek, Daniel Pink, etc.) So, agile coaches needed to get managers out of the way. If they stop coming to meetings, they will stop interfering.

The early creators of agile wanted the teams to feel safe. If the manager was there, the belief was that the team members would not feel safe to truly speak their minds because of the tradition of command and control. The tradition was the manager controls your raises and your reviews, and therefore that person has an unchecked power that they wield even though they do not know they are wielding it. When they walk into the room, they change the dynamic. There was and still is truth to that.

These are the three things that managers were told not to do. Imagine you are a manager and you are being told not to do these three items that you believe are core to your job. It can be remarkably frustrating. I have to admit. I was that guy. I told managers this myself. I told the chicken and pig story.

I have met these managers face to face. They are not only frustrated, but they are hurt. They are confused and resentful. All many managers want to do today is to help their teams. They want to support their teams. They want their teams to be successful and yet they are being told to stop attending, stop asking, stop doing the core things that you were told to do in management school.

With all the things they are being told not to do, and this is a huge thing for managers, no one tells them what to do. I cannot think of a time when managers have been told, "This is what your new role is." Unless it is just to say, "You are to serve the team and whatever the team needs, you give them." When you take away everything that they are supposed to be doing, it makes managers feel disempowered. They feel devalued, and they feel disenfranchised. You have taken away all of their authority and duties. They have nothing left to contribute.

Hiding Out In The Open

I have discovered that there is an answer to this. It was hidden out in the open the whole time, but we never saw it. We just weren't looking at the problem with the right perspective.

About two years ago I was working for a large software company in the Pacific Northwest (3,000, 4,000 people) and I was with a team six. We were doing much training trying to get the 800-900 plus software developers and the 150 or so managers trained, as well as helping them implement some technical Agile practices and Agile business processes. It was a typical Agile transformation.

Since there were lots of Agile coaches on site and many of them had experience with training Agile teams, and others of them had experience with executive coaching, I decided to look at the middle management since my experience and background came from being a manager and an Agile project manager.

I started by meeting with them holding cross-organization manager meetings, trying to glean from them what their problems were, what their issues were, how the transition was going, and how I could support them.

I had small cohorts that I was coaching. They would have two or three director level people working with one piece of the organization, and

I would coach that triad of directors and help them adopt an Agile mindset and Agile leadership approach.

It was in this year or so that I critically honed my thinking around Agile leadership and what it means to be an Agile manager. One of the early questions that came up with these managers was, what is the real role of an Agile manager? We had some great discussions amongst us as the Agile coaching team. We wrote an article for the internal blog, and it got me thinking. I did not feel satisfied with the outcome of that blog post. What you will read here I feel is significantly clearer and more empowering. I feel like this puts the manager in a new place, a better place than just being the team's lackey.

TIME FOR SOMETHING NEW

Around 2010 to 2015 through today, I am starting to see a shift. I see more and more leaders not steeped in command and control. This new crop of leaders has come up in an environment where they understand that what they need to have people engaged and creative not controlled and to limit variation. These are *first generation, digital immigrants*. People who have grown up with the technology revolution. People who had some computer when they were young and who have always known career paths that included something in the information technology realm. I up that way myself. I am a first generation digital immigrant.

Contrast this group with the group of middle managers who saw computers come into their business and completely change the way work is done, from manual adding machines and slide rules to pocket calculators and eventually personal computers.

First Generation Digital Immigrants have, for their whole lives, known tech careers. They have risen through organizations to positions of leadership. They may not receive explicit training that says, "People need autonomy, that they need engagement, and that they need be interested in the work they are doing to be at their most creative," they have understood that intuitively.

However, the approach to agile training has not kept up with this shift. Even I have found myself telling people who were doing the right things already to stop doing them and get out of the way. *However, they were not in the way in the first place.*

Telling managers what NOT to do did not sit well with me. **Maye this is you.** Maybe you have been trained in your career, knowing that command and control do not make sense for the knowledge work, but you do not have a good solid model to work from to move forward.

This book is exactly for you! Read on with enthusiasm!

The old style transformation

To break this old model of telling managers what NOT to do, we need to disrupt the old style of agile training. Sounds funny, does not it? "Old Style Agile Training." However, it is true. This approach has been around for 10 or 20 years depending on how you measure it, and it is time for a change.

This is the way I used to work with companies too, not so long ago. So, I am not trying to throw anyone under the bus. I am looking to start an evolution in agile coaching and offer hope to agile managers.

Let's look at a typical Agile transformation. The typical agile transformation follows three clear steps:

1. Train the teams
2. Train the managers
3. Coach the teams with embed-ded coaching

First, you train the teams for about two or three days. You have an Agile consultant or sometimes a coach who comes in. They do the training. The best ones pair up and do the training. They train the teams.

Then, they will do a half-day or a one-day manager and executive training where they bring all the managers and executives in to teach them about servant leadership. They tell them these things:

- Stop asking for status
- Stop assigning work
- Stop coming to meetings

Third, the coaches hang around for 6 to 12 months after this and coach the teams. These steps typify most Agile transformations. There are some benefits to this model. First of all, it is simple. It is very clear, very linear; people understand what they are supposed to be doing. They expect the coaches to come in. They have seen it before. They are doing a transformation. It gets quick results. Teams very quickly get up to speed using Agile practices. So, you see quick results.

A couple of the downsides

There are several downsides to the old model. However, I will only address a couple of them here. For more please just contact me, and I can point you to some resources that discuss the other issues. For now, let's look at the *Long-term dependence upon coaches* and *coaches as the experts*.

Longterm dependence on coaches

The first problem we will address with this approach is the high dependency on expensive consultants in the long term for the growth and agility of the organization.

The company is left relying on the consultants to coach their teams. They rely on them to train their teams for the long term. In many of these transformations there is, little or no manager or leader or executive coaching. In the best of circumstances, you will bring in an executive coach, and they will help the executives out, but that is not necessarily the rule, it is more the exception.

Additionally, if your organization is growing rapidly and you need to have large numbers of new employees trained, you will be beholden to these high paid coaches (like me in the past) to provide that training.

Coaches are the experts

In this model, another significant problem is that *coaches/trainers become the experts in Agile for the company.* The organization has no internal belief that they have the expertise or can be self-sustaining. They have a heavy reliance on this external group of people. And managers are often left wondering what their job is.

When the consultants leave what happens? Well, often the consultants do not leave. However, if they do what often happens?

Sliding Back To Waterfall

In the long-term, these organizations tend to slide back to waterfall ways. I am often called in these situations after they had an Agile coach or consult come in for training and coaching for a little while. The groups slide back towards traditional waterfall practices, often just with new names. So, you might have an organization that says, "We have a planning sprint, a design sprint, a development sprint, a testing sprint and a deployment sprint." You may have another team that says, "We get all the work done within one sprint and then in the next sprint, we do testing." These are waterfall practices done with little time boxes. They are not an Agile practice. I do not want to disparage these people or their situation. They may be experiencing some improvement by these mini waterfall It just is not optimal. Nor does it bring the hope and healthy atmosphere that is associated with a healthy organization.

I have speculated that this is often the problem, not only because the teams feel more comfortable with traditional waterfall practices, but also because you have taken the role of the manager away from them and not given them something equally as useful, meaningful and important to the organization with which to replace it. So, when the Agile coaches and consultants leave, the managers are still there. Over time, they subconsciously or consciously influence the teams to go back towards something they (the managers) are familiar with, something where they have a role and can be helpful. Again, in their heart of hearts, the managers of these teams want to help the team. When a good manager sees their team struggling, as all teams do when they start with practices, the good manager wants to help.

In the 2017 *State of Agile* survey that VersionOne puts out, there's one question that says,

Top 5 Tips for Success with Scaling Agile

1. Internal Agile coaches at 52%,
2. Executive sponsorship was 48%,
3. Consistent practices and processes were important to 41%.
4. Implementation of common tools 36%
5. Agile consultants or trainers 36%.

"Internal agile coaches," was the #1 critical factor for over half of organizations who were successful with agile. Shouldn't we focus on what is proven to be most effective in implementation? So, what are we doing to increase the number of **internal Agile coaches**?

There are some interesting issues with having internal Agile coaches. First, agile coaches are expensive. I found the following data about salaries for agile coaches on *payscale.com*, on July 24, 2017.

City	Median	High
San Francisco	$150,000	$280,000
Dallas	$120,000	$142,000
Washington, D.C.	$142,000	$208,000

Agile coaching is a highly specialized skill set, and they are compensated accordingly.

Now, one person cannot be everywhere at once, especially in something as intensive as coaching. Coaching is provided one on one or one on a small group. So, to coach a large organization, you would have to have several coaches. To effectively coach an organization of 800, you would need probably somewhere between five and eight coaches. A typical coaching engagement would include meeting with leadership, attending team events, such as; daily stand-ups, sprint planning, backlog grooming. Your agile coach would also meet with the product owners and scrum masters and meet with individuals. The range of coaching would include everything from change management for the transformation, executive coaching for the top leaders in the organization and technical coaching for teams and individuals.

You can see that this is a very busy job. However, can your company afford to add $150,000 (non-loaded cost[ii]) for every 100 people? If so, you can afford to add internal Agile coaches.

Is there an alternative? What if you could have internal agile coaches without that investment? What if you have the people already who can provide this internal agile coaching that 52% or the successful companies say is so important to their agile transformation. Moreover, what would you say if I told you that this person is YOU!

I created the Agile Formation approach for just this purpose.

The Agile Formation Approach

Let's step through the model first and then talk about the benefits and drawbacks of the agile formation approach.

The Agile Formation approach has four clearly defined steps.

1. Train the managers
2. Coach the managers
3. Train the teams
4. Coach the managers as they coach the teams

First, the consultant trains the managers. We use a process called the Flipped Classroom. Flipping the classroom is done through a combination of online video training and in-person training sessions and discussion groups. This model is used instead of traditional one time workshops so that content delivery can be optimized and you are not paying an expensive consultant to repeat the same thing over and over in all of the classes.

Second, the consultant provides coaching for the managers for one to three months. Notice here that the teams remain untrained. Only the managers have received training.

Third, the consultant **and** the manager co-train the teams. Teams receive access to the video training materials, just like the managers did. The in-classroom training is done to talk about implementation as well as to go through exercises that demonstrate the Agile practices in real-time so they can see the outcomes.

Fourth, is some ongoing manager coaching. Managers are provided coaching for four to six months or more depending on the needs of the individual managers. In this model, you do not need as many coaches because they are coaching the managers, not the teams.

NOT Train the Trainer

Agile Formation is not just a train-the-trainer model. Train-the-trainer does not work because they are trying to get a group of people with some expertise to a level of a consultant or coach quickly so that they can be the internal expert to train the teams. It takes longer than a workshop or class, and it takes the experience gained over time to become a coach or consultant

A professional educator and curriculum specialist helped develop The Agile Formation model. The processes for communicating, for supporting and for building leadership capacity within the organization follow a complex, multifaceted approach that prepares managers for coaching. We follow things like that Gradual Release of Responsibility[iii] model (GRR). We set up multiple support systems such as peer coaching support for the long term so that the managers are not relying long term on the consultants and coaches, but in the long term, they support one another.

Benefits of Agile Formation

There are numerous benefits to this model. First, the highest cost of the Agile Formation process is typically less than the lowest cost of the traditional model. The difference may range from 20% to 70% less than the traditional model. There's also a significant decrease in dependence on consultants especially in the long term because the consultant's job is to coach the managers and not the teams, so you do not need as many coaches. Building expertise in-house not only reduces costs but the internal employees will have a stronger tie to the organization. Part of the model is to set up peer coaching and peer cohorts so that over time the consultants are not needed at all, but the managers support one another in peer coaching.

Also, both managers and employees have long-term access to the video library so they can go brush up on material that they may have missed or heard but did not understand at the time. Managers do not have to teach Agile classes going forward. They only have to facilitate the practical application and implementation questions and the way things work in their company, which they are experts at in the first place.

Another benefit is in new employee orientation. New employee orientation of agility is greatly simplified because onboarding can be done using the online comprehensive video library system. New employees can watch those videos starting on day one and get up to speed quickly and not have to drag their team down learning Agile. Training the video modules can be reviewed anytime, stopped, rewound, re-watched, re-watched again, a week, several months later reinforcing multiple speeds and for multiple types of learning styles.

An additional and I believe the most significant benefit is that **managers are the long-term experts in agility for your organization.**

In this model, managers are central to the success of the effort. In other models, managers are left wondering what their job is in this new context. The Agile Manifesto was written 20+ years ago in a different time with different issues. The originators of the manifesto and a large majority of agile trainers started their careers as software developers, Many have never been managers and did not believe that management could enhance agility. I come from a management and project management perspective, so I just see a different perspective.

Drawbacks to Agile Formation

Now, of course, there are some drawbacks to this model. Organizations cannot just hand over the transformation. The managers have to get knee-deep in it. It is going to require many your managers so that they adopt an Agile mindset, Agile practices, and Agile leadership styles and learn they need to add a new tool to their professional development tool belt. That tool is agility, but with all the things that Agile approaches tell managers to stop doing. This model gives them something to do and something core, something as important as the things they were doing in the traditional model, maybe even more important.

Another drawback to this model is that to create high-quality internal leadership capacity requires longer to realize the benefit than the traditional model. The managers need a couple of months to get up to speed to be able to help facilitate the team classes. The timeline, of course, could be accelerated. However, the model is designed to work with the practical reality that managers are busy people and they do not have time to be taken out of their lives for significant intensive training. Additionally, studies have shown that extending learning over time and repeating concepts allows the training to sink into long-term memory.

21ˢᵗ Century Leadership

The traditional agile transformation model says managers need to stop assigning work, stop asking for status, stop attending meetings. Managers need to be servants to the team; ergo the team is now their masters. Now, I believe in servant leadership, but servant leadership is not *subservient leadership*. Servant leadership is a model where people are mutually submitted, mutually servants to one another. It only really works when people are servants to one another. If you just replace one commanding and controlling leader with another (Replacing the Executive with the team members), then you have not changed anything except who is giving the orders.

The picture is used most often to explain servant leadership is one that shows the triangle with the apex of the triangle pointing upwards and the boss is up there, and the people doing the work are at the bottom. The boss is at the top. In this model, authority is at the top, and the people who are doing the work are on the bottom. Then they talk about flipping the triangle where the boss is at the bottom. This person now we call a "leader" (not boss), and the team members are on the top. The problem with this model is you have only changed the orientation. You have only changed who's on top and who is on the bottom. You Have not gotten rid of or helped with the power structure problem.

There is an inherent bias in that last paragraph. Did you see it? Read it again before you go on.

Did you read it?

Did you see the bias?

It is subtle, but most cognitive bias is subtle. The tacit assumption implied is that *team members* are the only ones who do work.

In the first sentence "...*boss is up there, and* **the people doing the work** *are at the bottom...*" This bias is very subtle, but it is very common in many circles especially in agile circles.

Resist the bias. Realize that managers and executives are just as important as the individual contributor team members. They just have different scopes.

Executives need team members to execute on the higher level strategy, and individual team members need executives, to think globally, track and communicate strategy, to build the culture, and to maintain the focus of a cohesive organization, especially in large enterprise organizations. If there were no executives most large organizations will quickly deteriorate into chaotic, undirected, locally optimized but globally de-optimized clans.

The problem with single-servant-leadership where the CEO at the bottom is the servant of the teams is that now you just have a new master. The old hierarchical structures have an implicit power in the structure of the illustration. This relationship can be viewed as a one up/one down relationship. That is if you grab any two people on the chart, there will almost always be a relationship where one is perceived to have positional power over the other. This power persists even when in a context where the person in the one-down position has or should be taking leadership. Resisting this tendency is important.

I recommend that clients flip the triangle on its side and that you look at a model where you are mutually serving one another. A servant leadership model where everyone is a leader and everyone is practicing servant leadership.

Everyone is a leader

Everyone is a leader in an organization or should be. When you are in a meeting, and you are talking about strategy, you look to the CEO. You look to the executive team. They are the people who are leading at that point. In the same meeting when the conversation turns to sale

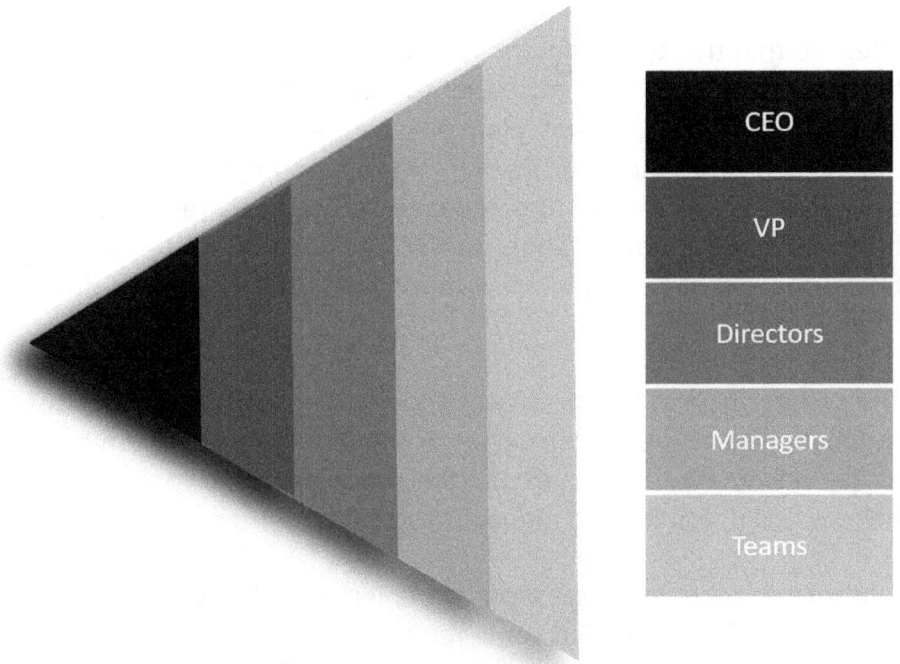

blocking defect in our product, you look to one of the helpdesk people. That helpdesk person becomes the leader at that moment.

If the conversation turns to databases and how the database is structured, the database designer or the database developer may become the leader of the conversation at that time. They need to be no less versed in the skills of leadership, and the understanding of servant leadership than the CEO needs to understand it. They are all leaders. We are all leaders at different times, and so we need to have mutual servant leadership, servants to one another.

In this way, we can look at the new role of manager. When they say, "When they take away status reporting and assigning work, what replaces it?" What replaces these activities is coaching and mentoring.

Remember these three statements?

- Stop Asking for status
- Stop assigning work
- Stop Coming to meetings.

I believe that these are admirable goals. However, they are goals. Just like I have a goal to have my daughter drive herself and her friends to school. However, I do not plan on just handing her the keys and hoping she does not kill anyone. My daughter needs training. My daughter needs to learn. She needs to be gradually released to drive, first with me her parent, then on her own with no distractions, then finally she might be, after a few months of driving, able to drive her friends to school.

The same is true of the statements above. Most Agile Coaches cut off the managers and put themselves in the place of the person to come to for information. Coaches do this because agile coaches do not believe it is possible for a manager to coach their people.

I disagree and believe that most managers are ideally suited to coach their teams. They just need some tools and training. Having managers coach their direct reports is not a new idea. Go to Amazon and search for "Manager Coach." You will find dozens of books that recommend the manager be a coach. NONE of them that I could find are by authors from the agile context.

I wonder why this is. I presume it is because most of the founders and drivers of the agile movement come from the ranks of individual contributors and in the past, they had a great conflict with managers. They still have the hangover to this day. The problem is gone and the only pain left is in their heads.

MANAGERS AS COACHES

According to a study, *the High Impact Performance Management: Maximizing Performance Coaching*, 2011 [iv], organizations that effectively prepare managers to coach are 130% more likely to realize strong business results from them. Thirty-nine percent stronger employee results through engagement, productivity and customer service. That is not Agile coaching. That is just general coaching that they were talking about in that study. Learning to be a skillful coach will help you step up your game. Maybe you think you will not see a 130% improvement but heck if you see half of that it is still 65% improvement. That is worth a lot in real money (in efficiency and better business results) but also in employee engagement and creativity.

Organizations across the world are seeing the value of managers being trained to coach their direct reports. I am not implying that managers need to be Agile coaches but managers need to have coaching skill. They need to understand what it takes to be a coach and what pieces apply to their job. So, in this next section, we will talk about three core elements, three core skills that will help you become a better Agile manager. An Agile coach has expertise that a coaching manager does not need.

- Deep knowledge the process of change for an organization

- Organizational design
- Excellent facilitation techniques
- Executive and manager coaching

Just to name a few skills. Could a manager benefit from these skills, sure but do they need them? Not really.

Adding the skills of an excellent coach to a manager's toolbox allows them to be even better managers. Coaching skills will greatly increase the effectiveness of any professional development planning, career growth planning, coaching thorough interpersonal problems on the job. Not only this but coaching skills make you a better manager and candidate for promotion or new positions.

I am a firm believer that every coach needs a coach. So managers should find coaches to work with to develop themselves. Zig Ziglar, the consummate salesman, and lifetime sales trainer said he had a real breakthrough in his first job, selling cookware door to door. That breakthrough came when a friend told him that the reason he was not selling anything was that, he had not purchased a set of the cookware himself. He was not sold on the product enough. So when his customers would come and say that they could not afford it or did not need it, he would subconsciously agree with them. When he purchased the cookware himself, he immediately started to sell more. The moral of the story: The first sale is always to yourself. If you are going to tell people that they need coaching, then you need to have a coach.

I have a coach, or depending on the time, multiple coaches. I find the best coach I can to help me with specific areas of growth and work with them for at least 6 12 months.

I coach managers and if you want to talk with me about coaching for you feel free to email me at joseph@whitewaterprojects.com or text or call (206)276-1386.

However, even if you do not contact me; GET A COACH!

3 Core Skills Of New Agile Managers

In this section, we will talk about three things you can do to help your organization be successful in their agile formation. First, we will talk about, **the coaching mind**. We will talk about **types of questioning,** and then we will talk about the **cycle of coaching** and how that all fits together.

Becoming a skillful coach requires adopting a uniquely different mindset from a traditional manager who used to tell their team members what to do and pushed for results. The coaching mind comes with the idea of getting results from a different perspective. We will discuss this perspective in the first section following.

Skilful coaches lead by asking good questions. There is both an art and science to asking questions. You will learn the six kinds of questions and the two big categories. You will learn when to ask them and when to drill down or drill up.

Finally, we will talk about the cycle of coaching. In this section, I lay out a common framework but adapt it to what I have found to work. You will learn how to follow the cycle of coaching, what you should be doing at each step and what your coachee should be doing.

Learning the skills of a coaching-manager can help you move from being a good manager to a great one. One of my clients, Collin Merry, said it best, "I used to think coaching was about me trying to be fixed. Joseph helped me realize that coaching is not about me being fixed it is about me becoming the best manager that I can. "

THE COACHING MIND

In this section, we will talk about six different elements that make up a coaching mind and what it takes to think like a coach.

- Coaching, Consulting, or Mentoring
- The need to believe in your coachee
- Trusting the process
- Holding space
- Emotional Intelligence
- Getting F.A.T.

So, let's get started.

Coaching, Consulting, or Mentoring

First, is it coaching, is it consulting or is it mentoring? What's the difference? You are probably wondering to yourself, "What's the difference?" What is coaching? What does it mean that you want me to be a coach to my team members now? Let's start by defining what coaching is not.

Consulting. If you have expertise that can help a client with a specific problem, you are consulting. You are asked to come in and help provide specific expertise and answers to a specific problem that the organization or the person is dealing with right now. This expertise may be highly specialized, or it may just be that you provide an external perspective. However, they are asking you for your expertise to help them improve as an organization in a specific area.

Mentoring, as a mentor, you are a more experienced person than the mentee. You are probably on the same career path as the mentee, and you are being asked to help provide them with your experience and wisdom as they encounter situations to guide them through and give them advice from your experience on what worked for you and what did not. Often, this is specific within the organization. It is a common practice to use mentors to groom leaders for executive positions. Mentoring others as they grow along a similar career path to the one you took.

Coaching is different from both consulting and mentoring. Your job as a coach is to bring out the best in the other person, to help them find their own best, not to give them who you are but to help them be the best that they can be. You want to help them be the best employee, the best Scrum master, the best database developer, the best designer, the best manager, baseball player or golfer. A coach does not have to have the same skills as the person who is doing the work. They have a process, and they trust that process. You as a coach help the coachee find the answer that they have themselves. You do not give them your answer. Now that is the strict definition of coaching.

Agile coaching is **all the above**. It includes a little bit of consulting, a little bit of mentoring, but the focus is usually through coaching.

Different than Co-Active Coaching. One very popular model of coaching is Co-Active coaching. If a coachee decides that doing 'X' is the best course of action, but you as the coach KNOW from experience that it is not, a Co-Active Coach would say, "Okay, let's try that and see what happens." A co-active coach brings no personal agenda except to make the coachee be the best most authentic them they can be.

However, do not be fooled or confused by the agile world's use of the word coach. Agile Coaches definitely have an agenda. It is to promote agile Practices, processes, culture, and leadership.

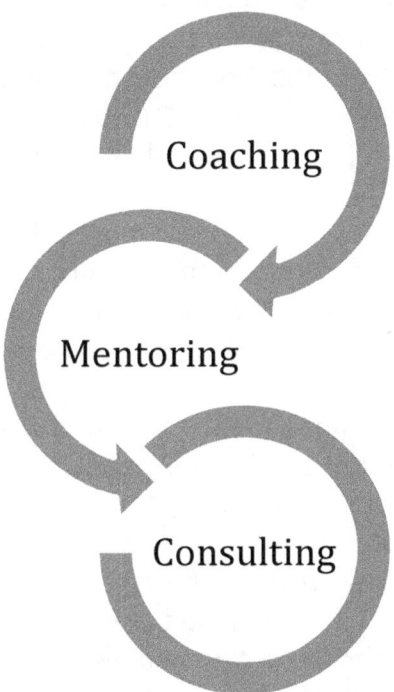

In the case that the person that they are coaching is unable to come to that conclusion themselves, agile coaches slip into mentor mode or consulting mode and usually in that order. So, the first model is to try and help the person conclude for themselves through coaching them to it. The second model is then to share your experience and your background from your wisdom that you gained in your time doing your work. If that does not work, then you are taking the role of a consultant and sharing with them this is the best practice. Now there's a lot more to it than just that, but that is the difference between coaching, consulting and mentoring. As I said, Agile coaching tends to be a mixture of all the above.

Believing in the Coachee

The job of the coaching manager is to help the coachee become the best them that they can be. To do that, a coach has to believe they can become a better them. A coach has to believe that people can grow can change. That talent can be learned. Remember the "Great Man" theory of leadership from the First Industrial Revolution. That model contends that leadership traits are NOT able to be learned. They are god given, and you are just born with them. Lucky you.

When you are a coaching manager you must believe that it is possible for a coachee to learn, grow and improve. A coach has to believe that strict, rigid mathematician brain of a person can if they want to, become an artist who can creatively express themselves.

Carol Dweck spent decades researching and creating the Mindset theory that shows that this fixed model of talents is not accurate: Fixed versus Growth mindset.

> "In a fixed mindset, students believe their basic abilities, their intelligence, their talents, are just fixed traits. They have a certain amount, and that is that, and then their goal becomes to look smart all the time and never look dumb. In a growth mindset, students understand that their talents and abilities can be developed through effort, good teaching, and persistence. They do not necessarily think everyone is the same or anyone can be Einstein, but they believe everyone can get smarter if he or she work at it." [v]

When I was a kid, people believed that IQ was fixed and there's nothing you can do about it. If you got your IQ measured and you had an IQ of 98, you would never be 100. You should just be happy that you are 98 and that you are not 60 and be happy with who you are.

Dr. Dweck's research found that that is not true. Things like IQ, things like skills, things like talent are not just innate. However, people with a fixed mindset believe they are. They believe things like "I am who I am. I have always been an introvert, so I will always be an introvert."

Alternatively, "I have always been good with my hands so I should be a mechanic, not a musician. I have never been artistic, and so I should not go into design." They believe that talent is innate, and because they are not currently perfect, they need to constantly promote their successes because this is as good as it gets.

Growth mindset says "No, we can change." Dweck's research showed and further cognitive science has confirmed that the brain is plastic, that it can reform. This concept is called neuroplasticity. We do not have just a limited number of brain cells. When I was a kid, they told me, "If a brain cell dies, it is gone forever." The number of brain cells you have when you are born is the number of brain cells you will have. If they die along the way from smoking pot or getting banged in the head, then you have lost them. So, do not lose too many or you will not be able to think anymore.

We know now that brain cells regenerate all the time and that your brain can learn and adapt and grow and change. You can learn all throughout your life, though the biggest growth is when you are a kid. You are still able to learn more as you go and grow throughout the rest of your entire life.

It is critically important that coaches believe the coachee is even capable of becoming, greater than the coach. So, check yourself:

- Do you believe that you can grow or is talent fixed?
- Can you get smarter or is your IQ fixed?
- Can you learn new skills?
- Can you grow?

If Dweck's Growth Mindset theory is true, what limits your potential right now? If the brain is plastic as science has shown it is if IQ is not limited (science has shown that it is not.) If talent can be learned, what's stopping you from being someone whom you want to be?

Believe in your potential and find out what's keeping you back. The job of the coach is to help the coachee find out what's holding them back.

Trust the Process

As a skillful manager-coach, you will have to trust the process. To trust the process, you must have a process. You must have a *macro process*, and you have to have a *micro process*. With that process, you have to know where you are in the process. We will talk about part of that process, the coaching cycle, later in this book. You need to know where you are at all times to understand what is next in the cycle, and what kinds of questions are appropriate at this point in the cycle.

Macro process refers to where is the individual or organization in their process toward their vision or goals. Are they just starting out? Are they in the process? Where in the process? On what parts of themselves are they working? Where are they in that process? The same applies to an organization. It is a lot more than we can go into in this short book.

The Coachee needs to trust the process too. If you do not trust it, they surely will not. You also need to make it safe for the coachee to fail. Part of trusting the process is making it safe for them. Safe for them to fail. Safe for them to explore. Safe for them to ask stupid questions. The old saying, "There is no such thing as a stupid question, or the only stupid question is the one that does not get asked." It is actually true. We encourage people to ask the questions that are on their mind. When I am facilitating a group, I talk about that a lot. I encourage people to ask the questions that are on their mind saying, "If it is on your mind, it is probably on other people's minds too. They are just not bold enough to ask it. Feel free and ask it for their sake, not for yours." That frees them up to be able to ask the question even though they feel sort of shy about it.

You can even pre-frame the question you are going to ask by saying, "Maybe somebody has the question X." Maybe somebody is thinking, "Is anybody else thinking why?" It is critical that as a coaching manager that you trust the process. If you do not trust the process, they will not trust the process. If they do not trust the process, you <u>will not</u> be able to coach them.

Holding Space

As a strong and capable leader/coach, you will need to learn to hold space at different times. Holding space is the idea of making that safe place, that place where people can mentally explore what's going on without having to worry about their surroundings.

As the person that is holding space, you need to be paying attention to the person for whom you are holding space. You need to be paying attention to the things that are going on around you. What's the temperature of the room? What are the other conversations that are happening? Can somebody hear what we are talking about right now? If so, is that going to impact the way the conversation goes? Pay attention to the surroundings. Do whatever it takes to allow the other person to be free of distraction, free of negative bias or positive bias, free of bias. You need to give them permission to act and permission to be free in their ideas and expressing ideas.

Lastly, to hold space, you have to be present. Being present is also critically important, not just physically present, but also mentally present. In concept it is simple, but it can be very difficult to be present to another person. Not thinking about how you are going to respond, not thinking about what's going to happen next, not thinking about your next meeting, not thinking about lunch, not thinking about the disaster that is happening with the rest of the team, but to be truly present to the person you are with takes significant energy.

As you are holding space, do not try too hard to ask questions or to help facilitate them as they are growing. Give them time to think. Give them time to reflect and contemplate and come to their own conclusions. Holding space is about helping the other person come to their own conclusions. Hand in hand with not trying too hard is *keeping quiet*. I continually run into managers who are very vocal. If your follower is not verbal, you need to wait on them until they are ready to speak. That does not mean filling the air with words until they come up with their thought. It means shutting up. I have coached executives to wait at least 10 to30 seconds by literally counting in their head, 1-One-Thousand, 2-One-Thousand...Every time I do the report back is that it was INCREDIBLY hard. However, it was rewarded with great insights from someone who normally does not contribute much.

In holding space, you need to be very clear that it is not about you right now. In coaching, it is all about helping the other person become the best them that they can be.

Get F.A.T.

Let's get FAT. Fat, no I do not mean put on weight. We are talking about getting fat, Joseph? No, I am talking about FAT as an acronym. You need to be **flexible, adaptable and teachable**[vi].

Things are going to go sideways, and you need to be FAT. You need to be **flexible**. You need to be able not just to be stuck with the plan, but that the plan is going to change. The plan is that the plan will change.

You need to be **adaptable** to those changes. Let them come. Let them change and adapt your approach to the new model. Adapt your thinking to what we are doing now. Being adaptable is the essential element of being agile. It is like wet to a fish. If you are not adaptable, then you cannot be agile.

Lastly, you need to be able to be **teachable**. It is important that as a coach you learn from the people you are coaching. You will find it if you have an open mind as you are doing it, you will find yourself learning from your coachees at least as much as they learn from the time they spend with you. So be FAT, be flexible, be adaptable, and be teachable.

POWERFUL QUESTIONS

A key tool in any coaching manager's toolbox is questions. We need to lead by asking good questions. No just any questions but Powerful Questions. A good facilitator does not ever need to tell you what to do. They will facilitate you getting there by asking you good questions. Not random questions, they are not shooting from the hip questions, but specific types of questions. Learning to ask good questions is a very complex and important skill. In this book, I will teach you briefly the **two big categories** of questions and **six different types** of questions. However, learning how to use questions and learning questioning skills is a lifelong journey. Being a good questioner helps you be a great manager.

Let's talk about some specific types of questions. There are two big categories of questions; **closed questions** and **open questions.**

Closed and Open Questions

A closed question, very simply, is a question for which there is an easy, quick one or two-word answer. A closed question says something like, "Do you think X? Do you want to do Y? Should we go to the..." Yes/no questions like this do not encourage conversation. They close down the conversation.

Both closed and open questions can be useful at different times. We will cover that briefly in the cycle of coaching, but just briefly here, note that closed questions tend to be helpful for bringing a conversation tighter and making it smaller. Open questions tend to be questions that encourage conversation. They encourage exploration. They encourage discussion. Open questions are not simple. You can't-answer them with just a couple of words or a sentence or two. Open questions need time and space to answer.

Six Types Of Questions

A key attribute of good coaching is real curiosity. Questions are a way to express our curiosity. If you can come to a coaching session with honest curiosity, not a mask of curiosity or pretend curiosity, but sincere curiosity about; where the other person is at, where they are coming from, where they are going, what they are thinking, how they are thinking, you will be able to dramatically help people by using a coaching approach.

Socrates, the infamous Greek thinker, executed for corrupting the youth was constantly questioning the authority of those in power in Athens. Socrates primarily taught by asking questions and letting the student figure it out. Scholars who study Socrates divided his method of questioning

- Questions about the question
- Conceptual clarification,
- Probing assumptions
- Probing rationale, reasons and evidence
- Questioning of viewpoints
- Probing implications and consequences

Questions about the Questions

First of all, we have questions about the questions themselves. These are the meta questions. Questions about questions ensure that you are asking are will eventually answer the right question. You will probably use some of these at the start of a new vision or goal to get headed the right way. You have probably heard of the person who put up a ladder and climbed and climbed with a heavy bucket of paint, only to find out they were against the wrong wall. That is what Questions about the Questions will help avoid.

You might use these when you feel like the answers your coachee is giving you are not aligned with what you anticipated or are inconsistent. First, they say yes, then they say no. This indecision is a hint that the ladder may be against the wrong wall. Do not wait to get to the top. Ask questions about the question right away and then recalibrate.

Questions about questions would be something like these:

- Why did you ask that?
- What is the purpose of that question?
- What does X mean?
- What does that question mean?
- How does the question apply?
- Why is that an important question?
- I am not sure I understand. Can you ask the question another way?
- Do we all agree that that is the question?

These questions help to clarify that we are on the same page. These get you on point to answering the right question

Questions of Clarification

These are questions like:

- How does this relate to our discussion?
- What do you mean by ...?
- What do we already know about X or how does X relate to Y?
- What is your main point?

These are questions for expanding the understanding of what a person has said if they have given you too short of an answer, an answer that was quick or you did not feel that they had delved into it enough or explored it enough. You might want to ask a question of clarification. Also, questions of clarification most often need to be used when you are merely curious.

Questions that Probe Assumptions

Questions that probe assumptions are another way of diving into that curiosity. These questions dig into the known or unknown beliefs that affect the coachee's filter or perspective. We ask questions like;

- What can we assume instead?
- How can you verify or disprove that assumption?
- How did you select that assumption?
- Is that always true?
- Why do you think that it is true here and now?

Good assumptions are those that cannot be proven or disproven they may only be believed to be true. With these questions, you are trying to help the person see the assumptions they have made that about the questions or statements they have had in response to your previous question.

We are often not aware of our assumptions. A good coach can help you become aware of the assumptions behind your unexamined beliefs or even your examined beliefs. They will help you examine them further. You can help people understand what they believe with what is their tacit belief behind the statements.

Questions of Rationale, Reason, and Evidence

Next are the questions that probe rationale, reason, and evidence. These are questions where you are looking for clarification of the proof. Here is the scientist coming to the question. You would ask questions like:

- Why did you say that?
- What are your reasons for saying that?
- Could you explain that further?
- Is that reason good enough?
- Is there reason to doubt that evidence?
- What could convince you differently?
- How did you come to that conclusion?

- What is your thinking behind that?
- Is there good evidence for that?
- What evidence makes you think that?"

These kinds of questions probe into a person's thinking so that we have asked questions about what reasons do they have to make the decision or to say the statement, what kinds of evidence have they seen or not seen? You are asking them questions, and all of them may be hard for people to answer. That is where *holding space* comes back in.

When you ask hard questions, known in coaching as *powerful questions*, people need time to answer them. Ideally, they will be able to answer during the coaching session, but sometimes they need even more time than that. Sometimes people need time to reflect and come back.

So, when you are asking questions like these, you want to hold space, be quiet, try not to reiterate unless they ask you to answer. It will be difficult. I have been there. I have had to hold my tongue when I wanted to state something again, especially if you are an extrovert, especially if you are a verbal person, you will have a hard time holding back. You need to hold back so the other person can process themselves.

Questioning Viewpoints or Perspectives

Next to questions where you are questioning of viewpoints or perspective, what lens are they seeing the world through? Questions like:

- Is there an alternative way to look at that?
- What would other people who have an opposing perspective say?
- Does anyone else see it differently?
- How are X's ideas different?
- How are George's ideas different or Sally's ideas different?
- Why have you chosen that perspective rather than another?

- What other perspectives are there on that or how would X react/respond to that?
- How would another person react/ respond to that, the person on the other side of a conversation?

These are useful when you are trying to help people who are in a conflict, helping them see the perspective of the other person. You want to help them get into the shoes of the other person. Is there another way of seeing that? What is the other perspective? Helping them see that the other person that is not irrational, they simply have a different perspective.

Questions Probing Implications

With these questions, you are helping them look forward into the future. All of the other questions, up to this point, have talked about looking at the situation and why the coachee responded the way they are proposing. Here we are talking about the future. We are probing about implications and consequences. Asking questions such as:

- What will happen if you pursue this approach?
- What are you implying by that?
- How do you think that will play out?
- If X and Y are true, then what else must also be true?
- If that happened, what else would happen?
- What would be the effect of that decision?

These questions help the coachee explore the future to look forward and see how their actions are likely to play out if they do what they say.

So that gives you some categories of questions. Learning to use those questions is going to be your journey from now until when you decide to stop being a coaching-manager anymore. Learning to ask good questions is a journey that I am still on myself. Now that we have got some questions, let's talk about the cycle of coaching and when those questions might apply.

5 Step Coaching Cycle

You can look at the 5 step coaching cycle from two perspectives. You can look at it from **your perspective of the coach,** and you can look at it from the perspective of **what the coachee is experiencing**. Let's look at it from the perspective of the coachee first. We will look at it from the Coaches perspective later.

There is a model called the GROW model developed by John Whitmore.[vii] Whitmore does a fine job explaining his model; I do not feel the need to explain it to you here. Just get the book. *Coaching for*

Performance, by John Whitmore. I like this model, and I use it. However, I add one more R at the end of it. So, for me, it is GROW+R model.

First, in the five steps comes setting **goals**. You want to set the initial goal of what we are trying to accomplish. This goal may be the goal for the session or a more long-term goal.

Next, you want to talk about **reality**. What is the current reality and how does that relate to the goal as it relates to those goals?

O for **options**. What are the options given our current reality trying to get to the goal?

Once you have discovered those options is the **will** to act. What am I willing to do? Given the **g**oal we are looking at, the **r**eality we have uncovered and the **o**ptions that we have identified and selected, what I am **w**illing to do to achieve that goal?

That is the GROW cycle. However, I have found it incomplete for as a long-term coaching model. As it stands, it is a linear model, and for a long-term relationship, we need a cyclical model.

So I have added one last step that cycles us back to the beginning. The last R that I have added to what's his name's model is **reviewing** because you always want to review what happened before. If we were starting a coaching session, we would start by reviewing what it was that you worked on, what it was you committed to in the last session. Then we would set the goals for the current session, because if you look at the last session and what you tried to do there worked well, then great. We can move on to something else, or we can talk about how to operationalize that thing that you tried.

It also may be that the coachee did not do anything toward their own self-committed goal. That is a whole new opportunity for growth.

If the experiment did not work, then they need to either scrap it and come up with a new idea or move on to a new topic. Reviewing past goals first is important.

They will be reviewing, and you will be the accountability for that review. You are helping the coachee be accountable to themselves. You are not holding a hammer over their head. You are helping them remember that they committed to this.

The questions are simple, "Did it work?" If it did work, then, "How do we make this the new normal?" If it did not work, then they need to come up with something different. Simply asking, "What else can you try?" "Do you want to try something else?"

This is the typical coaching framework I use with my clients every day. If you have never used a coaching model like this, where you do not lead the conversation but facilitate the coachee as they learn on their own, it will be awkward and uncomfortable at first. You will be afraid that they will not come up with the right ideas or the best ideas. You will be afraid that there will be an awkward silence. However, let me assure you it will not be that bad.

Here is a little exercise to reassure yourself that it will not be that bad. Take out a piece of paper right now. On that paper, list all of the things that could go wrong. Define the worst-case scenario.

OK did you make that list? So. What is the worst that can happen? I mean if you screw up and do not do something right. Oh and as you do remember that when a coachee is REALLY going off the rails, that you can always shift to mentoring, and if that does not work you slip over to consulting. So, you are not without recourse. What is the worst that will happen? Nothing that is life threatening because you will not let it get there.

From the Coaches Perspective

All the while you are going through the 5 step coaching cycle you will be paying close attention. Holding space and asking questions. However, you will also be doing two more things. **Listening** and helping them come up with ways to **practice**.

Listening

There are three levels of listening, and those are first is listening for a break in conversation so I can say my piece. This is the lowest level of listening, and you do not want to be doing that here. You want to be actively listening, actually listening.

Level-one listening is about you and not about them. Remember that coaching is always about the coachee, helping the coachee be the best them they can be. So, we do not want to be doing level-one listening in a coaching session.

Level-two listening is listening for understanding. Listening for understanding is what we commonly think of as good listening. Level-two listening includes the concepts of active listening where you are responding back, rephrasing what someone has said where you are paying attention and being intent upon the other, trying to understand what they are doing and what they are thinking and what they are saying. It can be quite difficult to be truly present to another person and listen to what they are saying.

Level-three listening is called global listening. In global listening, you are not only paying attention to their words, and you are certainly not paying attention to yourself. You are watching things like body language. You are listening to how they say what they say not just that they said it. You are paying attention to the micro expressions[viii] of a person's face that give clues out as to what they are thinking and feeling. It is global, paying attention to the whole situation.

You are paying attention to how the temperature of the room might be affecting their thinking right now. Is the coachee feeling tired because the room is too warm? Are they feeling uptight because the room is too cold? Are they feeling hurried or cloudy thinking because they Have not eaten? Pay attention to more than just the person where they are at now. You are paying attention to the whole situation. This is global listening.

Listening can be very difficult. You need to understand why you are listening, what you are listening for, how you are listening, and what level you are practicing. Trying to be present and being present is not thinking about the thinking. So, for it to become intuitive, you should be kind to yourself. You have to catch yourself when you are off and gently allow yourself to go back. Do not beat yourself up. It takes time to learn. It takes practice. Being present takes practice. Helping another person is not easy work.

You also when you are listening want to be listening and there exploring the current reality, you want to be paying attention to the balance. Is the coachee only seeing the negatives or are they only seeing the positives? We do not want the Debbie Downer, and we do not want Pollyanna. We do not want someone whose glass is always half empty, and we do not want the person whose glass is always half full. We want to talk about the emptiness of the glass and the fullness of the glass. We want to talk about the good things that are possible and the challenges you may incur along the way.

Practice

Together you will develop ways for the coachee to practice their new behaviors. Practice may be as simple as keeping a journal of their daily activities and tracking the times they were able to implement the new experiment and times they were not.

Whatever the model is, it is important to create opportunities to practice even in artificial situations so that when the real situation comes, the new behavior will be as natural as riding a bike.[ix]

Dallas Willard, a theologian, has a great illustration of the need to practice in his book, *Spirit of the Disciplines*. He is talking about spiritual disciplines, but the illustration is as valid;

> "Think of certain young people who idolize an outstanding baseball player. They want nothing so much as to pitch or run or hit as well as their idol. So what do they do? When they are playing in a baseball game, they all try to behave exactly as their

favorite baseball star does. The star is well known for sliding head first into bases, so the teenagers do too. The star holds his bat above his head, so the teenagers do too. These young people try anything and everything their idol does, hoping to be like him they buy the type shoes the star wears, the same glove he uses, the same bat. Will they succeed in performing like the star, though?

"We all know the answer quite well. We know that they will not succeed if all they do is try to be like him in the game—no matter how gifted they may be in their own way. And we all understand why. The star performer himself did not achieve his excellence by trying to behave in a certain way only during the game. Instead, he chose an overall life of preparation of mind and body, pouring all his energies into that total preparation, to provide a foundation in the body's automatic responses and strength for his conscious efforts during the game. Those exquisite responses we see, the amazing timing and strength such an athlete displays, aren't produced and maintained by the short hours of the game itself. They are available to the athlete for those short and all-important hours because of a daily regimen no one sees. For example, the proper diet and rest and the exercises for specific muscles are not a part of the game itself, but without them the athlete certainly would not perform outstandingly.

"Some of these daily habits may even seem silly to us, but the successful athlete knows that his disciplines must be undertaken, and undertaken rightly, or all his natural talents and best efforts will go down in defeat to others who have disciplined themselves in preparation for game time. What we find here is true of any human endeavour capable of giving significance to our lives. We are touching upon a general principle of human life."[ix]

As Dr. Willard's example so eloquently says. We have to practice new behaviors so that they will be natural when we need them. Learning to be present is no different.

Bonus Tip

OK, so I just wanted to provide you with something extra, really special and useful tip. I learned this from my wife

From actively disengaged employees to the swiftly disenchanted millennials, getting employees engaged is a critical issue for retention, satisfaction, and productivity. What do you do? What can a leader do to affect so many people to reel them back and engage them? Sure there are the traditional ideas: Give away free sodas, have Friday beer events, or take the team bowling, but these ideas take significant planning and cost money you do not have.

There is one thing you can do today that will cost you nothing and will directly address one of the top reasons that people at all levels leave their organizations. From CEOs to janitors, the most common reason that people leave their business is the same; **they do not feel appreciated.** So, appreciate them! However, it needs to be honest and specific appreciation. You cannot be general or grudging about it.

However,…it can be hard. However…you have significant employees. However…they are all doing different things. How can you tell each one of them on a weekly basis something specific and heartfelt that you genuinely appreciate about them? Besides, you say, I am just not the kind of person that hands out compliments left and right. Verbal acknowledgment is one of the strongest forms of recognition and is completely free. However, it can be hard to do.

Well, I have just the trick for you!

The solution: Pay-it-forward appreciation

Try this super simple solution that will make you the most appreciating manager in town (it has a bonus too):

Step 1: Ask one of your team members, "Can you help me out? Who are two people who have done something this week that you truly appreciate?" They will name a couple of people.

Step 2: Go to each of those people, individually. As part of your conversation, maybe as you are leaving, share the appreciation from the other co-worker. "Oh, by the way, Bob said he appreciated how you handled the recalculation module."

Step 3: Then ask them the same question, "Can you help me out? Who are two people who have done something this week that you genuinely appreciate?"

It is a positive pyramid of appreciation. This method has subtle benefits. This type of reinforcement is possibly more powerful than you coming up with something yourself because you are sharing something that someone else said when the other person was not even around. You can appreciate everyone on your team with honest and heartfelt appreciation. You did not have to make anything up; it is all true, and it is specific. There is also an added benefit that you receive from this method. It builds relationships in two different directions. It builds bonds not just between you and the person you spoke the appreciation to, but it also builds a bond between the person who told you they appreciated someone and the person they identified.

Appreciation will not change the work. It will not make hard work easy but it will make it easier **to be at work.** When we feel appreciated, we want to feel inspired and want to work. Now that I think of it, it can make hard work seem easier.

WHAT'S NEXT?

I sincerely hope you have enjoyed this book. These concepts have genuinely made a difference in my life and the lives of my clients. If you found this helpful, I know you are definitely going to enjoy my brand new program called **The Agile Manager's Inner Circle.**

You have purchased this book. You have read it. You know that these practices will improve the effectiveness of your teams and your effectiveness as an agile manager. That is why you are going to want to be a part of The Agile Manager's Inner Circle.

If you want to be seen as the linchpin in the success of your organization's agile formation. If you want to help, your company get every penny from its investments in its agile... If you want to dramatically improve the productivity and engagement of your teams... If you want to learn how to become the coach for your team and be critical to their growth into high performing teams...

Then **The Agile Manager's Inner Circle is just for you.**

Walkthrough

Here is a rundown of what you are getting with the Agile Manager's Inner Circle. The mind map below will be the framework of what you are getting when you become a member of the Agile Manager Inner Circle.

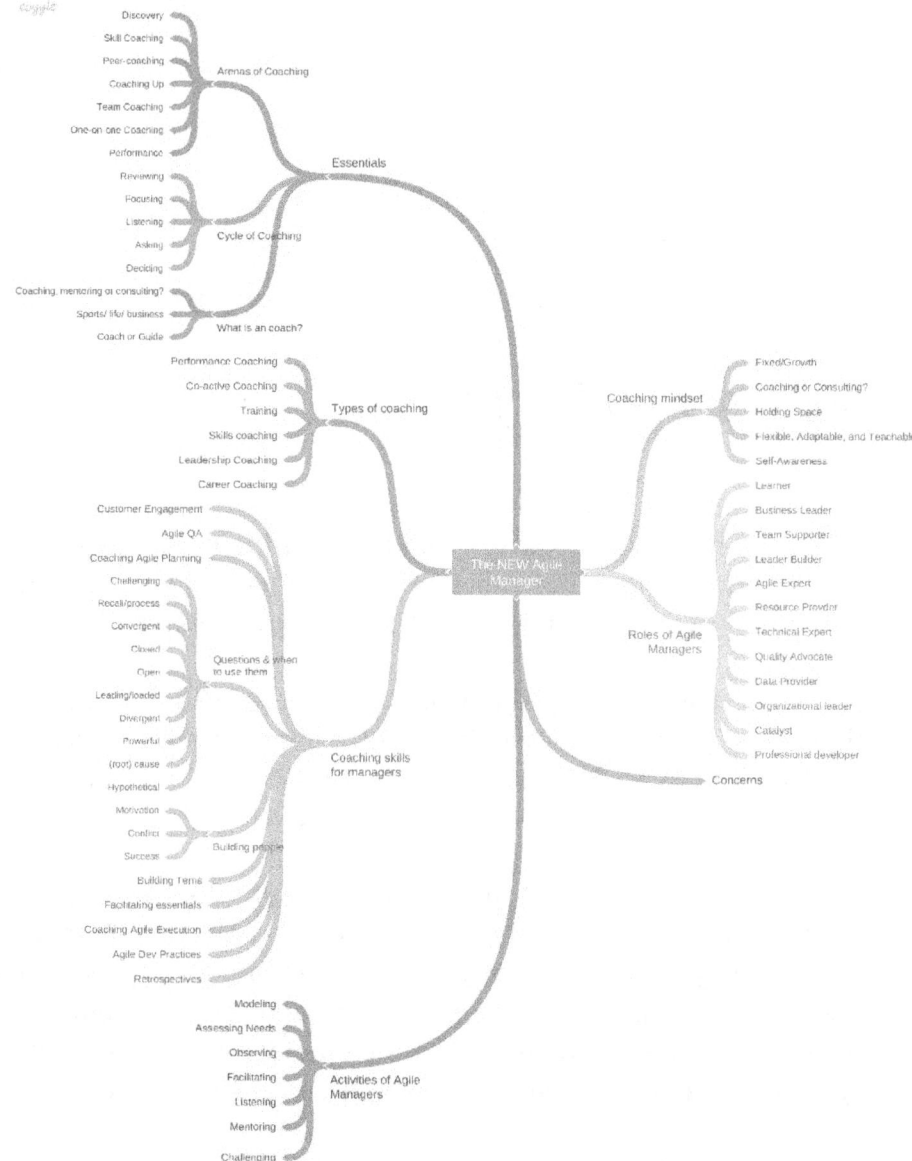

- You will have access to a closed group of like-minded managers.
- Live video conferences where we will discuss YOUR questions.
- We will have role play coaching of difficult coaching moments

- As a member of the Agile Manager Inner Circle, you set the agenda.
- Deep dives into managing with self-organizing teams.
- Develop your unique approach to coaching.
- Explore new ways to maximize your team's capabilities
- Anything you need, you do it together.
- Open Q&A every other week.
- Plus other surprise bonuses.

The value you are getting when you join the community is enormous!

However, the real value you are getting is in becoming the source of agile wisdom for your organization. Agile Coaches typically charge about $2,000 per day. If you hired one to work with your team for one month that could cost about $40,000! For one month! A full year of agile coaching would be $450,000! Almost half a million dollars. Agile Coaching is expensive, and I am not saying that you can completely do away with agile coaching. Your organization may still need some coaching for the actual formation, but for ongoing support of your teams, you should not need someone whose exclusive job is agile coaching.

So here is what I want you to do now. Go to;

http://bit.ly/AgileManagerIC

and join the Agile Manager's Inner Circle.

Contact me anytime at

Joseph@whitewaterprojects.com

Alternatively, call me at

206-276-1386

End Notes

i https://en.wikipedia.org/wiki/Fourth_Industrial_ Revolution

ii Loaded cost would include the cost of payroll taxes, insurance, benefits and miscellaneous costs

iii https://en.wikipedia.org/wiki/Gradual_release_of_responsibility

iv http://marketing.bersin.com/high-impact-performance-management.html

v "Stanford University's Carol Dweck on the Growth Mindset and Education". OneDublin.org. 2012-06-19.

vi Thanks to Brandon Brazee for this acronym FAT, Flexible, Adaptable, Teachable.

vii http://amzn.to/2wo7QZO

viii https://en.wikipedia.org/wiki/Microexpression

ix https://www.cio.com/article/2952410/it-strategy/how-cios-can-be-champions-of-culture- change.html

x Dallas Willard, Spirit of the Disciplines, HarperOne; Reprint edition (May 5, 1999)

www.ingramcontent.com/pod-product-compliance
Lightning Source LLC
Chambersburg PA
CBHW050240230526
45470CB00005B/2037